My Rainbow Baby

Caitlin G Johnson

My Rainbow Baby
Copyright © 2020 by Caitlin G Johnson

All rights reserved. No part of this publication may be reproduced, distributed, or transmitted in any form or by any means, including photocopying, recording, or other electronic or mechanical methods, without the prior written permission of the author, except in the case of brief quotations embodied in critical reviews and certain other non-commercial uses permitted by copyright law.

Tellwell Talent
www.tellwell.ca

ISBN
978-0-2288-3977-4 (Paperback)

Before you came along there was another:
an amazing gift like you, a son or daughter.

After a few weeks, something felt wrong.
The doctor told Mummy baby wasn't growing strong.

My tummy was hurting, and so was my heart.
For Mummy and Daddy, it all fell apart.

We planted flowers and trees at
our favourite place. We would love and
remember our sweet baby in a special space.

Mummy's tummy felt like a heavy and loud storm.
Until you, my treasure, started to form.

With you in my belly, it feels like a rainbow.
It's my pleasure to carry you everywhere I go.

I promise to adore every smile and laugh, every change of clothes and every muddy bath. I'll love your feet thundering on the floor; each time we play will be better than before.

I'll help you grow and learn and flourish; you're my earth-side treasure to love and nourish. While we miss our very first gift, your gorgeous rainbow heals that rift.

www.ingramcontent.com/pod-product-compliance
Lightning Source LLC
LaVergne TN
LVHW071734060526
838200LV00032B/492